Everything
You Need to
Know About

Depression is not "all in your mind." It is a crippling illness that affects millions of Americans.

Everything You Need to Know About *Depression*

Eleanor H. Ayer

The Rosen Publishing Group, Inc.
New York

Published in 1994, 1997, 2001 by The Rosen Publishing
Group, Inc.
29 East 21st Street, New York, NY 10010

Revised Edition 2001

Library of Congress Cataloging-in-Publication Data
Ayer, Eleanor H.
Everything you need to know about depression / Eleanor H.
Ayer .— Rev. ed.
p. cm. — (The need to know library)
Includes bibliographical references and index.
ISBN 0-8239-3439-X (library binding)
1. Depression in adolescence—Juvenile literature. 2. Depression
in children—Juvenile literature. 3. Teenagers—Mental health—
Juvenile literature. [1. Depression, Mental.]
[DNLM: 1. Depression—Popular Works. WM 171 A976e 2001]
I. Title. II. Series.
RJ506.D4 A94 2001
616.85'27—dc21
                                                      2001000013

Manufactured in the United States of America

Contents

Introduction

Sasha had just moved to a new town with her family. Sasha's mom loved her job, and her sisters, Charlotte and Sophie, made new friends, but Sasha felt lonely. No one understood her. The kids at school seemed mean and false. They teased her for dressing like a "freak," laughed at her when she spoke, and deliberately gave her the wrong directions. She felt misunderstood. Sasha didn't want to ruin her family's happiness by complaining so she suffered in silence. Soon, she stayed home from school a lot, insisting she had a stomachache. Her brain felt numb. Sasha's days in a fog were disrupted only by the occasional flood of inexplicable tears.

We all get the blues sometimes. But when those feelings hang on for weeks or months, it's probably more than just a bad mood. It may be an illness called depression.

Depression describes a person's condition when he or she feels sad, discouraged, and hopeless. Often, a depressed person has trouble functioning. He or she might feel exhausted all the time and have difficulty thinking clearly or quickly.

Recent studies have shown that more than 20 percent of adolescents in the general population have emotional problems and one-third of adolescents attending psychiatric clinics suffer from depression. Depression affects 20 percent of all women, 10 percent of all men, and 5 percent of all adolescents worldwide. It is the most common psychological problem in the United States, afflicting nearly 18 million people each year. "Depression is a disorder most commonly associated with adolescent suicide," says Dr. W. Michael Nelson, chairman of the department of psychiatry at Xavier University in Cincinnati, Ohio.

But most depressed teens never get the professional help they need. Some people believe that only "crazy" people seek the help of a mental health expert. But if you're depressed, or if you know someone who is, serious depression isn't something that

Sometimes, a depressed person feels like he or she is in a fog and is unable to focus or concentrate.

you can simply "get over" or "break out of." There is nothing wrong with seeking professional help.

If you can't seem to shake the blues—or if you know someone who can't—you do not have to feel lost or hopeless. Depression can be treated and, in most cases, cured. This book will help you learn about depression, its causes, and what to do (and who to call) to help yourself or a depressed friend.

Chapter 1

What Is Depression?

Roz knew her mother was upset with her. It was a firm rule in their house that chores had to be done before everything else. But lately, whenever she tried to do anything, Roz's stomach hurt. It wasn't just an excuse to get out of work. But her mother thought it was.

Roz and her mother began arguing more and more. Roz's mom was especially annoyed by Roz's attitude. "You're so negative, no one can talk to you anymore," her mother yelled. The more they argued, the worse Roz's stomach felt.

Who Has Depression?

Depression is remarkably common. More than 5 percent of Americans—some 18 million people—suffer from clinical depression at any given moment. Another

Friends, relatives, and doctors often miss the subtle signs of clinical depression.

5 percent experience mild symptoms or feel blue. At least one person in six has a serious depressive episode during his or her lifetime. For some people, depression is caused by an imbalance of chemicals, or hormones, in the body. A person's mood sometimes depends on the chemical makeup of those hormones. If they are out of balance, the person can become depressed.

Experts say that 70 percent of people treated for depression will experience the illness again. Usually, those later periods of depression are less severe than the first. One out of every three people who have suffered from depression never has another serious problem with it.

What Does It Feel Like to Be Depressed?

Like Sasha, people who are depressed tend to feel sad all the time. But depression can affect people differently. It can make some people feel tired all the time, yet they may have trouble sleeping at night. Others might lose their appetites or may suddenly start overeating.

When you're depressed, nothing seems to work out the way you'd hoped. Whatever you do seems to go wrong. Even if it doesn't, you can see only the bad things, and you start to focus on them. After several failures, you begin to think nothing will ever work out. "See—why did I even bother trying?" you might ask yourself. "I knew I was going to mess things up." A depressed person can feel hopeless, helpless, and, worst of all, alone. It becomes easy for depressed people to feel trapped by their troubles.

It Can Happen to Anyone

An enduring myth is that people with depression cannot function, when actually 72 percent of depressed individuals remain in the workforce. Some are taking medication or some other form of treatment. Many try to carry on in spite of their deep, emotional pain. Many famous people have struggled with clinical depression, including President Abraham Lincoln, journalist Mike Wallace, comedian Rodney Dangerfield, poet Sylvia Plath, statesman Winston Churchill, artist Georgia

When you are depressed, you may feel as though you are a failure who cannot do anything right.

Many successful people have suffered from depression, including Abraham Lincoln and Winston Churchill.

O'Keefe, actor Rod Steiger, and writers William Styron, Virginia Woolf, Ernest Hemingway, and Mark Twain.

Types of Depression

◎ **Reactive depression is a temporary depression, such as depressed feelings that arise because of a specific life situation or transition. Depressive reaction is called an adjustment disorder with depressed mood. The symptoms can be severe, but usually subside within two weeks to six months and do not require treatment.**

◎ Dysthymia is known as minor chronic depression. It is similar in its symptoms to depressive reaction, but it lasts much longer, usually at least two years.

◎ **Major depression** is a serious condition that can lead to an inability to function or even to suicide. It is a cyclical illness, so although most patients recover from their first episode, the recurrence rate is high—perhaps as high as 60 percent within two years and 75 percent within ten years. Major depression often appears and disappears spontaneously and is seemingly unprovoked. It might begin as a depressive reaction following a loss or trauma, and can intensify and evolve into a full-blown depressive episode. The episode may also disappear spontaneously, usually within six to twelve months, though treatment is often needed to achieve full control of symptoms.

◎ **Bipolar disorder (or manic-depressive disorder)** involves major depressive episodes alternating with periods of wildly energetic activity. About 1 percent of the American population experiences bipolar disorder in a given year.

◎ Atypical depression is less constant. A person with this condition might seem deeply depressed for a few days, then fine for a while, or anxious and irritable.

◎ Seasonal affective disorder is often referred to as "winter blues." A reaction to lack of sunlight in winter, mild or major depression develops in late autumn and clears up in early spring. This condition becomes more common as distance from the equator increases.

◎ Postpartum depression results from the enormous hormonal changes that occur when pregnant women give birth and begin the challenges of caring for an infant. Some two-thirds of new mothers experience this form of depression. However, about 10 to 15 percent become clinically depressed. And about 1 in 1,000 becomes so severely depressed that the person needs to be hospitalized.

Friends, relatives, and family doctors often miss the subtle signs that point to a need for professional help. The various types of depression don't have firm, clear boundaries. Often it takes professional judgment to decide when normal grief or an adjustment disorder has become a more serious form of depression. This is

Winter can cause a form of depression called seasonal affective disorder, which is a reaction to lack of sunlight.

a big reason why clinical depression often goes undiagnosed and untreated. Lacking a diagnosis and help, some people attempt suicide. People often overlook depression because so many accompanying symptoms mask it. Depression often manifests itself physically in the form of physical ailments such as headaches, back pain, irritable bowel syndrome, chronic fatigue, anxiety, sleep problems, and shortness of breath.

To help doctors diagnose mental health problems, including depression, the American Psychiatric Association (http://www.apa.org) publishes a professional handbook, *The Diagnostic and Statistical Manual of Mental Disorders (DSM)*. This manual lists the signs and symptoms of depression in its various forms.

Chapter 2

How Can You Spot Depression?

While diagnosing depression can prove tricky, depression does have clear biochemical roots that affect nerve cells in the brain. Severely depressed people have unusually low levels of several brain chemicals: the neurotransmitters serotonin, dopamine, and norepinephrine. Neurotransmitters carry messages from one nerve cell to another. The unusual levels of these chemicals may be inherited, which may explain why depression tends to run in families. Although researchers have yet to discover a depression gene, many suspect a genetic connection.

Deep emotional losses can also trigger the biochemical changes that cause depression. Profound trauma in early childhood—the death of a loved one, a bitter divorce, physical or sexual abuse, or other very disturbing experiences—can cause depression later in

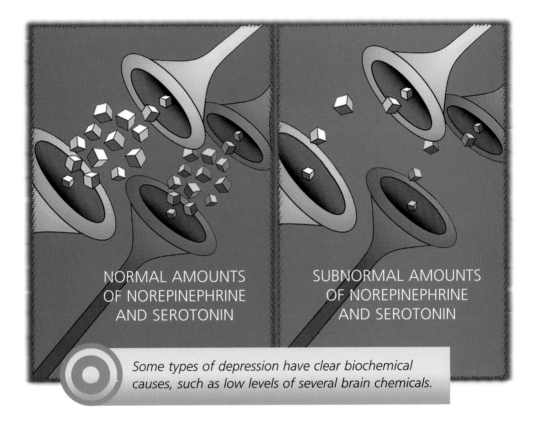

NORMAL AMOUNTS
OF NOREPINEPHRINE
AND SEROTONIN

SUBNORMAL AMOUNTS
OF NOREPINEPHRINE
AND SEROTONIN

Some types of depression have clear biochemical causes, such as low levels of several brain chemicals.

life. Just as frequently, though, the brain chemistry of depressed individuals changes for no apparent reason. People who are well adjusted and well loved can also become seriously depressed.

Are You Depressed?

◎ Do you feel sad all the time?

◎ Are you not interested in friends or activities that you used to care about?

◎ Are your grades suddenly dropping?

◎ Are you frequently tired and out of energy?

◉ Do you have difficulty concentrating?

◉ Do you have trouble sleeping, or are you sleeping more than usual?

◉ Do you have thoughts about suicide or thoughts about harming others?

◉ Do you often eat too much or not enough?

If you can answer yes to any of these questions, you may be depressed.

People suffering from major depression show definite symptoms or signs. It may or may not be obvious to friends and relatives that the person has a problem and needs help. A person may live with depression for years, never realizing that he or she has an illness that could be cured. Many of the symptoms of minor depression are the same as those of major depression. The difference lies in how severe the symptoms are and how often the person experiences them.

Minor Depression Vs. Major Depression

When it seems that there are more negative days than positive ones, this may be the start of minor depression. Minor depression can become serious because many people are not aware that they are suffering. They assume that their "down" moods will pass. But if left untreated, minor depression can turn into a major depression.

Time is the biggest test. If the "down" mood goes away after a good night's sleep or in a few days, the person is probably not depressed. If two or more of the following signs are present all day, every day, for two weeks or more, however, the person could be suffering from major depression.

What to Look For

◎ Thoughts or suggestions of death or suicide

◎ Feelings of guilt or worthlessness

◎ Lack of physical and mental energy

◎ Lack of interest or pleasure in most activities

◎ Too much or too little sleep

◎ Rapid mood swings

◎ Argumentativeness

◎ Problems concentrating, making decisions, or solving problems

◎ Trouble making or keeping friends

◎ Absence of goals in life

◎ Trouble finishing projects or doing even simple tasks

◉ Change in appetite: rapid weight loss or weight gain

◉ Upset stomach, headache, or numbness in parts of the body

◉ Hyperactivity

◉ Slowness of speech

◉ Failure to pick up after oneself

◉ Hallucinations (strange, unreal perceptions)

◉ Pessimism (always expecting the worst)

Sometimes a person suffering from a mental illness shows it by feeling physically sick.

Cindy's mother began to worry when her daughter complained constantly about her health. After nearly six weeks of poor school attendance and fatigue, Cindy's mother took her to a doctor. When the doctor could find no physical reason for Cindy's ailments, he suggested that she see a therapist. He believed Cindy was suffering from depression. Her mental condition was causing her to be physically ill.

Chapter 3

What Causes Depression?

As discussed in the previous chapter, the physical basis of depression involves neurotransmitters in the brain. In the brain, the nerve cells do not touch. There are microscopic gaps between them called synapses. For a nerve impulse to travel from one nerve cell to another, the sending cell releases a tiny amount of one of the neurotransmitters, which transmits the signal to the second cell, and so on around the body. After a nerve impulse has been sent across a synapse, special enzymes clear away the neurotransmitter so that another impulse may be sent. Depression is strongly associated with abnormally low levels of certain neurotransmitters.

There is some proof that certain forms of depression may be inherited. Genes, tiny parts of cells that carry traits from parents to children, are the "recipe" for a new person. If you are born with genes that cause the body to produce too much or too little of certain hormones, you will have a chemical imbalance. This imbalance may put you at greater risk for depression. Manic-depression, or bipolar disorder, is the kind of depression that is most often inherited.

According to major studies of depression in children, it takes more than just genes for a person to suffer from depression. Life experiences affect a person's risk of developing depression as much as genetics. Research indicates that if genes have caused an imbalance of chemicals in your body, it may take only a little stress or physical illness to bring on depression. But if your body has a normal chemical balance, you may be able to handle much more stress without feeling depressed.

Before Depression Strikes

Depression doesn't come on suddenly. First, a person goes through a period of long-term stress. The stress may last for weeks, months, or even years.

Dwayne was a responsible kid and a good student who was well liked by his teachers. He had

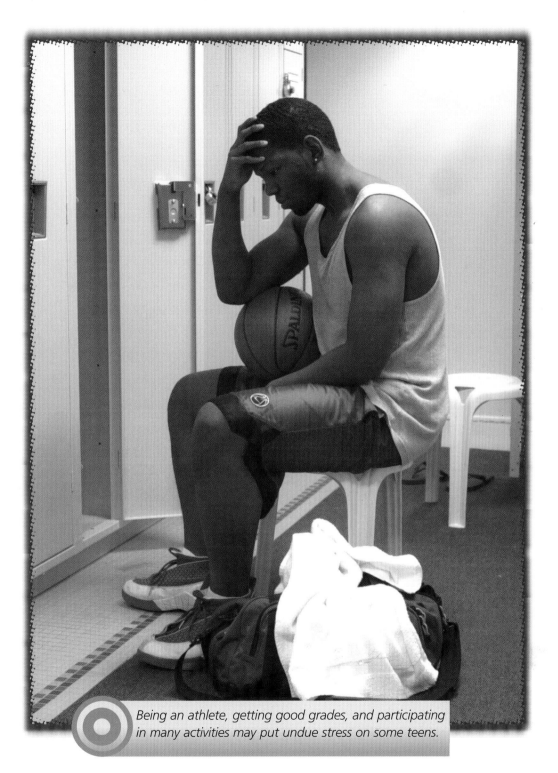

Being an athlete, getting good grades, and participating in many activities may put undue stress on some teens.

many friends, belonged to a religious youth group, was captain of the basketball team, and was a part-time cashier on weekends. His parents were very proud of him and praised him constantly. It seemed as if Dwayne could do no wrong.

The stress of always having to be the "perfect" teenager was hard on Dwayne. After months of living with this stress, he began to feel overwhelmed. "Dwayne, can you be in charge of the junior class car wash next weekend?" "Dwayne, are you running for student council president?" "Dwayne, can you write an article for the school paper about the basketball team's winning season?" Everyone expected him to take on additional responsibility.

Dwayne became so overwhelmed by all of his obligations that it seemed as if he had lost control of his life. He had so many things to do that he no longer did any of them well. He had trouble remembering the simplest tasks. He jumped from one thing to another, never finishing anything. Soon Dwayne began feeling helpless and hopeless. He was often in a bad mood. The smile and good words he used to have for people vanished. In the privacy and quiet of his room, he often cried.

How the Body Reacts to Stress

When a person is under stress, the body reacts in stages. The first stage is worry or alarm.

Alec was under a lot of stress in football. As the quarterback, people expected him to lead the team to victory. Every day the coach worked with him. After practice he would remind Alec, "I'm counting on you, son." In Alec's mind, a voice kept saying, "Don't blow it, Alec. They'll all hate you if you lose the game." Because he was worrying so much, Alec's heart rate increased. His blood pressure went up. He was stressed.

In the second stage, Alec's body tried to resist, or fight, the stress. If he had been able to resist, he could have brought the stress under control. But Alec could not resist. All he could do was worry about what might go wrong. "What if?" he kept asking himself. Constant worry made him do poorly in practice. When his coach got upset and yelled at him, Alec's stress increased.

Since Alec was not able to resist stress, his body went into the third stage, exhaustion. By the day of the game, Alec was so tired he could hardly get out of bed. He hadn't slept well nor eaten properly for days. His mind and body were simply worn out.

What Causes the Body to Develop Depression?

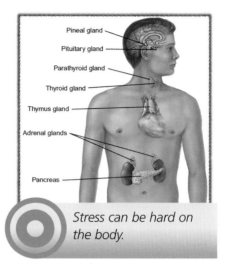

Pineal gland
Pituitary gland
Parathyroid gland
Thyroid gland
Thymus gland
Adrenal glands
Pancreas

Stress can be hard on the body.

When stress becomes too great, our body goes into the "fight or flight" response. Our brain gives us two choices: We can run from the thing that is causing the stress (flight), or we can stand firm and face it (fight). To prepare us for the choice we make, our body produces hormones. These chemicals help us react under pressure. One common stress-fighting hormone is adrenaline.

Stress is very hard on the body. It is particularly hard on the endocrine system, which is in charge of producing hormones. Under constant stress, the endocrine glands get out of balance. They produce too much or too little of the different chemicals our bodies need.

The master gland of the endocrine system is the thyroid. This complex gland affects many body functions, especially growth. It works closely with the adrenal gland, which produces adrenaline for fight or flight. A person whose thyroid is too active may show signs of mania. He or she may be hyperactive and have trouble sleeping. When the thyroid is under-active, the body can go into depression. The person becomes exhausted. He or she has little energy.

When our hormone balance is upset, it has a great effect on our emotions. A chemical imbalance in our body can change our mood, our mind, and our feelings.

Where Long-Term Stress Can Lead

Think about riding a bicycle hard and rough, day after day, jumping off curbs and making fast stops from high speeds. Constant stress and pressure will shake the bicycle's bolts loose and cause its frame to bend or break.

The same things happen to people under stress. Constant strain, and wear and tear on the body and mind cause a breakdown, both mental and physical. Stress can—and very often does—lead to depression. When that happens, only a trained specialist, using the proper therapy, can help a depressed person get well again.

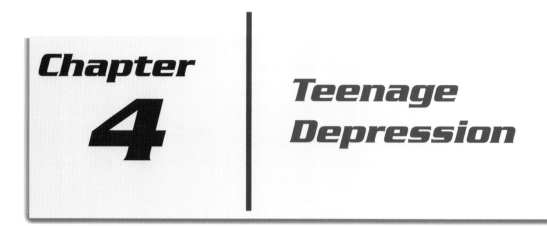

The teenage years are an emotional roller coaster, even for adolescents who are loved and well adjusted. For young people who are neglected or abused, being a teenager can be a nightmare. Is it any wonder that many teens experience significant symptoms of depression?

Parents, teachers, friends, and relatives often find it difficult to recognize and deal with depression. Teens often express their depression in ways parents may not expect. Instead of symptoms such as apathy, lethargy, withdrawal, hopelessness, and unusual sleep patterns, depressed teens tend to be intensely irritable, have angry outbursts, experience problems, and show destructive behaviors such as alcohol or drug abuse. In the United States today, depression among young people is so common that it's considered an epidemic.

Some teens express depression by having violent outbursts or acting out in a destructive manner.

What Causes Teenage Depression?

The most common type of depression in teens is reactive depression. This is the kind caused by some outside event in a person's life. Often the teenager has no control over the event, which may involve:

◉ Death or divorce of parent(s)

◉ Conflicts or violence at home

◉ Physical illness or disability

◉ The end of a close friendship

◉ Problems in school

◉ **Pressure to succeed**

◉ **Peer pressure**

Many teenagers work through their problems with the help of friends and family. Eventually, they feel better. But those teens who don't have continued love and support may not be able to overcome the stress. Teens without support are the ones who may continue to suffer from depression.

What Makes Teenage Depression Different?

Adolescence can be a particularly difficult period. Teens are in the midst of attempting to establish an identity independent of their families. Teens also experience major hormonal changes, often prompting emotional highs and lower lows. Any and all of these factors can lead to deep emotional reactions. Other prominent teen stresses include identity issues, struggles among peer groups, and establishing sexual identity.

Teenagers who suffer from depression often act out instead of acting sad. Their behavior may be wild and angry. They don't seem to care what happens to them or anyone else. Getting into trouble at home, at school, or with the law may be their way of showing that they have problems.

Teenagers often express depressive symptoms in unexpected ways, such as committing crimes like stealing or vandalism.

Many times, adults don't look at depressed teenagers as children who need help. They see them as juvenile delinquents who should be punished.

Symptoms of Teenage Depression

The adolescent years are a time of great change, both in mind and body. Teens are trying to become independent. Most rebel against authority in some way. For that reason, the early signs of depression are often ignored. These are some common ways that teenagers show depression:

◎ **Long-term boredom or a lack of interest in any activity**

◎ **Acting out, getting into trouble at home, at school, or with the law**

◎ **Drug or alcohol abuse**

◎ **Taking unnecessary risks**

◎ **Increased "accidents," some done on purpose to hurt oneself**

◎ **Sexual misconduct**

◎ **Poor performance in school, athletics, etc.**

◎ **Loss of friends; isolation**

◎ **Headaches or other physical complaints**

◎ **Talk of suicide**

Most adolescents go through periods of being bored with life, misbehaving, or taking risks. But when this kind of behavior goes too far or happens too often, it could be a sign of depression.

Sherry became depressed when her father told her to break up with her boyfriend. Sherry had been going out with Jake for nearly two years and was sure she loved him. They had had sex several times. The thought of losing him was more than she could bear. Sherry stayed angry with her father and refused to do what he wanted. Late at night, she would sneak out of the house. She started skipping school and let her grades slip. One night as she lay in bed, Sherry made a plan. She decided she would become pregnant. Then what could her father say?

Sherry stopped using birth control and had a baby nine months later. But there were parts of her plan that didn't work the way she had imagined. Jake got scared when he heard he was going to be a father. He moved out of state to live with his mom. Sherry's father threw her out of the house. Now Sherry was on her own, left to raise her child alone. Depression had changed Sherry's life forever.

Chapter 5

When Depression Is in Your Home

The misery of depression extends beyond those suffering it to their families and friends. If you are close to someone who is depressed, try not to take it personally. He or she has an illness. Like a patient struggling with diabetes or cancer, a depressed person has a condition that is beyond his or her control.

People often feel guilty around others who are depressed. If their efforts to cheer the depressed person fail, they feel like a failure. Children of depressed parents need reassurance that the illness is not their fault. Children, in particular, may blame themselves for their parent's sadness and feel guilty. They need reassurance that their parent's depression is not their fault, so they, too, do not become depressed.

Depressed people can often frustrate and alienate those around them. Experts say that if you live with someone who is depressed, there is an 80 percent

If you are close to someone who is depressed, don't take it personally. A depressed person has a condition that is beyond his or her control.

chance that you will become depressed, too. That means eight out of ten people who live with a depressive become depressed themselves. It can be very difficult to conceal your impatience when a close friend or relative does not return your e-mails or phone calls, rarely gets out of bed, or acts completely self-absorbed.

Many experts believe that reaching out does make a difference. Social support improves treatment results in other illnesses. It can help a person who is depressed as well. Try to show that you care. The depressed loved one may not respond to you, but depressed people notice and appreciate the effort.

How to Deal with Depression

Even though a depressed person may not want to talk, it's important that he or she does talk. It might seem scary to approach a parent or sibling who is depressed, but communication is the key to getting the help he or she needs. If you can, talk first with another family member about your concerns.

◎ **Tell the person you care and that you are worried about him or her.**

◎ **Talk honestly about how you feel.**

◎ **Don't take it personally if the depressed person doesn't want to talk or gets angry with you.**

◎ Always be ready to listen whenever the depressed person is ready to talk.

◎ Be supportive and show that you want to help. Provide information about depression and places to go for help.

◎ If you aren't sure what to do—or if you can't talk with your parents—try to confide in another adult you respect and trust, like a teacher, a guidance counselor, or a relative.

What NOT to Say to a Depressed Person

Sometimes well-meaning friends and relatives make things worse by talking to a depressed person in the wrong way. Depression is serious and complicated. There are no quick answers. Many parents feel responsible for their child's depression. But parents who respond to depression in any of the following ways will only make matters worse:

◎ Pretending the depression is a "phase" the person is going through.

◎ Making the person feel guilty—"You're bringing down this whole family!"

◎ Punishing the person for acting out.

◎ Constantly pushing him or her to live up to goals that are too difficult.

◎ Lecturing the person about things he or she already knows—"You've got to stop looking like you lost your last friend!"

If you have a depressed friend, it's important to talk with the person about the problem. But watch what you say and how you say it. Here are some "don'ts" to remember if you expect to keep the lines of communication open:

◎ Don't label or criticize—"Quit being such a grouch."

◎ Don't preach—"Now, you listen to what I'm going to tell you."

◎ Don't pretend the person's problem is not that bad—"Just get a good night's sleep. Things will be much better in the morning."

◎ Don't question or nag—"Come on, I know something's bothering you. Tell me what's on your mind."

◎ Don't be too kind or too harsh—"You're sick. Just stay in bed and let us take care of you."

- Don't suggest a simple solution to a serious problem—"Let's go to a movie and forget your troubles."

- Don't accuse the person of pretending to be sick—"Get off it. I know you're just doing this to get attention."

Be Kind to Yourself

If you live with a depressed person, you may have mixed and confused feelings toward him or her. Try to be honest with yourself. Admit that sometimes you may feel:

- Hatred toward the person for bringing problems into your life

- Anger because the person seems to be acting this way on purpose

- Fear about what may happen if the person doesn't get better

- Guilt that you may have caused the person's depression

- Jealousy that the depressed person gets so much attention

- Frustration because things never seem to get better

Speaking with a therapist can often help those suffering from depression and those affected by the depression of others.

To help you deal with your feelings, you need to continue the activities that are important to you, and stay in touch with good friends and relatives. Tell them you're having a hard time. If you can, consider seeking counseling for yourself.

To Guard Against Depression

⊙ **Stay involved with other people.**

⊙ **Avoid becoming isolated.**

⊙ **Pursue hobbies and interests.**

⊙ **Strengthen other family connections.**

Chapter 6

When Depression Becomes Severe

Suicide is now the second leading cause of death for those ages fifteen to nineteen. Each year 250,000 teens attempt suicide and 2,000 actually kill themselves. Since 1960, teen suicides have doubled. Girls are more likely to attempt suicide, but boys are four times more successful at killing themselves, usually with guns.

Risk Factors for Teen Suicide

- ◎ Delinquency and social problems
- ◎ Drug abuse
- ◎ A family disrupted by death
- ◎ Divorce
- ◎ Abuse
- ◎ Parental neglect
- ◎ Homophobia

This last factor, homophobia, an irrational fear of, or discrimination against, homosexuals, is still often over-looked. As many as 30 percent of teens who commit suicide are gay. Realizing you are gay as an adolescent can be terrifying if your community, family, and friends are not supportive or act openly hostile.

Certainly, many teens have experienced one of these risk factors. So why do some turn to suicide? Susan Swedo, M.D., of the National Institute of Mental Health (NIMH) focused on identifying those teens serious about committing suicide. She found two key factors, hopelessness and a firm belief that life is not worth living. If teens believe that they have no future, suicide is a real possibility. Sometimes, friends and loved ones refuse to discuss suicide for fear of putting the idea into a person's head. Suicidal thoughts come from within; they are a reaction to great pain.

Warning Signs of Suicide

How can you tell if someone is truly planning to commit suicide? You can't always be sure. That's why any talk of suicide should be taken seriously. A comment like "The world would be better off without me" can be a warning sign. The most dangerous thing a person can do is ignore the warning or assume that his or her loved one isn't serious. Here are some warning signs to watch for in a depressed person:

◉ Constant talk of death or dying

◉ Withdrawal from friends and family

◉ Giving away prized possessions

◉ Direct or indirect threats of suicide ("After I'm gone . . . ")

◉ Presence of "suicide tools," such as guns, rope, pills, etc.

◉ Very sudden happy mood or improvement in a depressed person's condition

Heeding the Threat

Many parents worry that talking openly with a child about suicide will cause him or her to consider it. Usually, just the opposite is true. Talking honestly to a depressed person is best. Attempts at suicide are often a cry for help.

Many young people who attempt suicide once will try it again. To keep this from happening, it's important to show the depressed person love and support. But there are important things to do right away to help a person who is severely depressed.

◉ Remove guns, rope, knives, pills, etc., from the home.

◉ Have them seek treatment immediately.

⊚ If possible, take part in the therapy or counseling.

⊚ Do not leave the depressed person alone for long periods of time.

People who are serious about killing themselves go about suicide differently than those who do not really want to die. Seriously depressed people plan their suicides carefully. They prepare themselves and get their affairs in order. Usually, they warn people of their plan. Many times they leave a note telling why they want to die, and then carry out the suicide alone.

If you or someone you know is contemplating suicide, you can get help now from a suicide prevention hotline. Many hotlines are accredited by professional organizations such as the American Association of Suicidology, Rehabilitation Accreditation Commission (CARF), and the Joint Commission on Accreditation of Healthcare Organizations. Also, refer to the contact information listed in the back of this book.

Chapter 7

Getting Help

Though depression is treatable, many Americans continue to believe otherwise. Although patients usually respond well to treatment, relatively few people get help when they need it. Among depressed adults, only one in three is treated. While it is estimated that about 80 percent of people with depression can improve their mental health with psychotherapy, medication, or both, people continue to believe that treatments do not work.

Certainly, our society continues to have negative stereotypes of those suffering from any type of mental illness. A recent study conducted by Michael M. Faenza, president and CEO of the National Mental Health Association, revealed that the entertainment and news media continue to portray individuals with mental illness negatively. The study asked more than 1,000 people, "How does the media impact the public's perception of mental illness?" More than half believe those with mental illness are portrayed negatively in movies, television shows, and books. Television shows and movies frequently depict those with mental illnesses as dangerous and addicted to drugs and alcohol. Further, news shows often note the presence of mental illness when reporting on criminals but remain silent about mental illness in the lives of people receiving positive press. Unfortunately, these stereotypes perpetuate the belief that depression is untreatable.

What Therapy Can Do

Depression is a disease that requires long-term care. Verbal therapy occurs over several sessions or meetings. These sessions are usually helpful for several reasons. Some mental health experts believe that depression often occurs when a person is trying to avoid dealing with a painful memory. Mental health experts can also determine what kind of therapy will help their patient most.

Choosing the Right Therapist

Recovery from depression is often assisted by an effective therapist. When faced with the difficult task of

Television shows, movies, and books frequently depict those with mental illnesses as dangerous criminals.

choosing a therapist, it helps to be guided by your own level of comfort. Choose a doctor whom you can trust.

◎ **Psychiatrists.** These are licensed doctors who have completed medical school. They treat diseases of the mind and can prescribe medications.

◎ **Psychologists.** These are mental health professionals who have gone through many years of training but are not licensed medical doctors. They cannot prescribe drugs. Like child psychiatrists, child psychologists specialize in treating children and teenagers.

◎ **Social workers.** These trained professionals work with groups or families. They deal with a wide range of problems, from family violence to drug and alcohol abuse. When choosing a social worker for depression therapy, be sure he or she has experience in treating mental illness.

Good therapists are truthful about what will happen during therapy. They talk with the patient about the kind of therapy they will use, how the sessions will be run, and what to expect.

Different Types of Therapy

The appropriate therapy depends on the patient's personality and condition. Most therapists recommend one of four kinds of verbal therapy.

◎ **Cognitive-behavioral therapy.** Also called cognitive restructuring, cognitive-behavioral therapy teaches people to recognize and correct depressive thinking. For instance, should you perform poorly on a math test, you might think, "I'm stupid and I'm no good at math!" Constant negative thinking can cause a person to slide deeper and deeper into self-hatred. Cognitive-behavioral therapy attempts to stop the mind from turning minor upsets into catastrophes. With cognitive-behavioral therapy, the reaction changes to "Okay, I made a mistake. Fortunately, I can ask my teacher for help." A National Institute of Mental Health study found that after sixteen weeks of cognitive restructuring training, 51 percent of those with mild to moderate depression reported significant improvement.

◎ Psychoanalysis. During this kind of therapy, patients look inward at their own personalities to understand themselves. The therapist helps patients find reasons for their problems and ways to overcome them. This type of treatment can last for several years. An NIMH study also showed that after sixteen weeks of psychoanalysis, 55 percent of those with mild or moderate depression reported significant improvement.

◎ Group therapy. This can be especially good for teenagers. People of the same age group meet in counseling sessions to discuss their problems.

◎ **Family therapy. This is treatment for the whole family, but it centers on the depressed person. It helps family members live comfortably with the depressed person by relieving stress and tension in the household.**

When Different Treatment Is Needed

Sometimes verbal therapy is not enough to treat depressed persons with predominantly physical symptoms. Doctors may also prescribe one or more antidepressant drugs.

Most therapists want to see their patients in therapy sessions so they can monitor their progress while taking antidepressant drugs. If a patient is severely depressed, however, drugs may be used first, before therapy is started. Doctors prescribe several types of antidepressant drugs, including the following:

◎ **Selective serotonin reuptake inhibitors (SSRIs). These drugs increase the effectiveness of serotonin in the body. Serotonin is a neurotransmitter, which transmits messages from one cell to the next. In depressed people, neurotransmitters do not work**

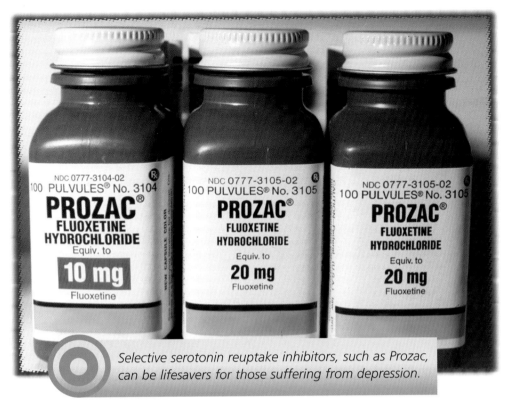

Selective serotonin reuptake inhibitors, such as Prozac, can be lifesavers for those suffering from depression.

as effectively. Prozac and Zoloft are two kinds of selective serotonin reuptake inhibitors.

◎ Tricyclics. Tricyclics increase the effectiveness of serotonin and another hormone called norepinephrine, which is also a neurotransmitter. Tricyclics include imipramine, desipramine, amitriptyline, and nortriptyline.

◎ Monoamine oxidase inhibitors (MAOIs). These antidepressants are rarely used, usually only if SSRIs and tricyclics don't work. People treated with MAOIs have to restrict their diets and cannot eat certain fermented foods, such as cheese and wine. MAOIs are usually quite effective.

◎ **Lithium.** This was one of the first anti-depressant drugs. Today, it is used mainly for controlling the mood-swing symptoms of manic-depression or bipolar disorder.

There is also electroconvulsive therapy (ECT), commonly called shock treatment. In ECT, the patient is put to sleep with drugs, and an electric shock is sent into the brain. ECT is usually given only to severely depressed people, especially if they are suffering delusions. Because ECT relieves depression more quickly than drugs, it may be lifesaving for people who are suicidal.

Nondrug Therapies

◎ **Exercise.** A large amount of research shows that aerobic exercise elevates mood, relieves anxiety, and improves appetite, sleep, and self-esteem. Studies show that it also normalizes chemical imbalances in the brain linked to depression.

◎ **Herbal medicines.** Several medicinal herbs have antidepressant effects. The most powerful is St. John's Wort, a natural SSRI and mild MAOI. In addition, kava-kava, ginkgo, and SAM-e may also help.

◎ **Dietary supplements.** Certain vitamin deficiencies, notably B_1, B_2, B_6, and folic acid, can cause depression. However, keep in mind that too much of certain vitamins can also cause problems.

◎ **Alternative treatments.** The United Nations World Health Organization recognizes acupuncture as an effective treatment for moderate depression. Other helpful treatments include massage therapy, music and art therapy, yoga, and meditation.

The Downside of Drug Therapy

Strong antidepressant drugs can affect a person's whole body, causing side effects such as upset stomach, constipation, dryness of the mouth and eyes, a drowsy "drugged" feeling, headache, and weight loss or gain.

Sometimes, side effects from a drug can affect a person's health even more seriously. They may cause blurred vision, a change in heart rate, faintness, skin rashes, or seizures. In extreme cases, a person may become mentally confused or even hallucinate—have unreal, dreamlike visions. Suffering side effects from an antidepressant drug can be very discouraging, especially if your doctor frequently changes your medications.

Making Therapy Work

A doctor or therapist can only help depressed people get better. Patients must decide for themselves that they want to improve. Depressed persons must believe that recovery is possible, yet must admit that there are no guarantees and that effective treatment is different for everyone. People recovering from depression must learn to be able to recognize changes in their moods. Being aware of abrupt mood changes can signal a need to get help immediately.

Therapy works best when the whole family gets involved. If a depressed person feels that he or she is alone, it may make him or her feel worthless. When therapy continues for a long time, it may be easy to get discouraged.

Therapy can help a person change certain behaviors or ways of thinking. But the depressive is not the only one who may need to change. Other family members and close friends must look at their own behavior, too.

Drugs must be taken only as prescribed. This may mean regular medication for a number of weeks or months. If depression is chronic, however, the doctor may put the patient on an extended drug therapy program to fight the pattern of habitual depression. Some patients dislike being dependent on drugs to regulate their lives, but it is important that they understand what is prescribed and why it is prescribed.

Depression Is a Curable Illness

With the right therapy, as many as eight out of ten people can recover from their depression. More than half of those who begin therapy will see results within a month to six weeks.

Devon went through therapy for more than five weeks before she felt any change at all. "My therapist kept telling me to stick with it, but it was difficult. Then one day, I woke up and the fog that had been around my brain all these weeks seemed gone. I could think clearly. Suddenly, I was excited about going to school and about seeing other people. I still had many months of therapy ahead of me, and many hard times, but I'll never forget that day that I seemed to turn the corner."

Devon knows that she could suffer from depression again in her life. An estimated 70 percent of patients who recover from depression relapse. But, like Devon, they know that it is treatable. There is hope.

Glossary

adrenaline Hormone produced by the body during periods of stress.

antidepressants Drugs prescribed by a doctor to treat depression.

anxiety Extreme state of nervousness or fear.

attitude Way of thinking or acting.

compulsion Uncontrollable urge to do a certain thing.

counselor Person who offers advice and help with special problems.

delusion False, persistent belief sometimes caused by mental illness.

depression Mental illness in which sadness and gloom overwhelm a person's normal daily life.

endocrine system Body system in charge of producing hormones.

epidemic Large number of cases of a disease that happen at the same time in the same area.

gene Part of a body cell that carries traits from parents to children.

hallucination A mental image of something that is not really happening, but seems real.

hormones Chemicals in the body that help it to grow, stay healthy, or respond to stress.

mania State of high, unnatural excitement or enthusiasm.

manic-depression (bipolar disorder) A form of mental illness in which a person's mood swings quickly from intense sadness to high excitability.

neurotransmitter Chemical that transmits messages from one cell to the next.

obsession Strong fixation on an idea.

panic attack Sudden, uncontrollable fear or anxiety in a situation.

psychiatrist A doctor who treats mental illness.

psychoanalysis The study of people's personalities, emotions, and subconscious minds, developed by Dr. Sigmund Freud.

psychologist A person who has studied human behavior and treats problems of the mind.

stress Extra pressure or demands made on the body or mind.

suicide The intentional killing of oneself.

symptom Sign or indication of something.

synapse The point at which a nervous impulse passes from one neuron to another.

therapist A person trained to help patients recover from an illness or injury.

therapy Treatment for a disease or condition.

Where to Go for Help

If you need help right away, you can call these confidential, twenty-four-hour hotlines:

Boys Town Suicide Hotline (for boys and girls)
(800) 448-3000

Hit Home Youth Crisis Hotline
(800) SUICIDE or (800) 999-9999

Organizations
National Alliance for the Mentally Ill
Colonial Place Three
2107 Wilson Boulevard, Suite 300
Arlington, VA 22201-3042
(800) 950-NAMI (6264)
Web site: http://www.nami.org

National Depressive and Manic-Depressive Associations
730 North Franklin Street, Suite 501
Chicago, IL 60610-7204
(800) 826-3632
Web site: http://www.ndmda.org

National Foundation for Depressive Illness, Inc.
P.O. Box 2257
New York, NY 10116
(800) 239-1265
Web site: http://www.depression.org

National Mental Health Association
1021 Prince Street
Alexandria, VA 22314-2971
(800) 969-NMHA (6642)
Web site: http://www.nmha.org

In Canada
Canadian Mental Health Association
2610 Yonge Street, 3rd Floor
Toronto, ON M4S 2Z3
(416) 484-7750
Web site: http://www.cmha.ca

For Further Reading

Beckelman, Laurie. *Depression*. Parsippany, NJ: Crestwood House, 1995.

Carter, Sharon, and Lawrence Clayton. *Coping with Depression*. Rev. ed. New York: The Rosen Publishing Group, Inc., 1995.

Chelsea House Staff. *Depression*. New York: Chelsea House Publishers, 1996.

Chiles, John. *Teenage Depression and Suicide*. New York: Chelsea House Publishers, 1991.

Gelman, Amy. *Coping with Depression and Other Mood Disorders*. New York: The Rosen Publishing Group, Inc., 2000.

Herskowitz, Joel. *Is Your Child Depressed?* New York: Warner Books, 1990.

Roleff, Tamara, ed. *Teen Suicide*. San Diego, CA: Greenhaven Press, 2000.

Wolpert, Lewis. *Malignant Sadness: The Anatomy of Depression*. New York: Free Press, 2000.

Index

About the Author

Eleanor H. Ayer is the author of several books for children and young adults. She has written about many current social issues of interest to teenagers. Her recent topics include stress, teen fatherhood, teen marriage, and teen suicide. Ms. Ayer holds a master's degree from Syracuse University with a specialty in literacy journalism. She lives with her husband and two sons in Colorado.

Photo Credits

Cover © Ron Chapple/FPG; pp. 2, 8 © Index Stock; pp. 11, 13, 17, 25, 31, 37, 42 by Antonio Mari; p. 14 © FPG International (left); p. 14 © Associated Press (right); pp. 19, 28, 53 © Custom Medical; p. 33 © Paul Conklin/Pictor; p. 49 © The Everett Collection.

Layout and Design

Thomas Forget